FENG SHUI

MADE EASY

4	9	2
3	5	7
8	1	6

FENG SHUI

MADE EASY

Richard Craze

GODSFIELD PRESS

Published in 1999 by Sterling Publishing
Company, Inc. 387 Park Avenue South,
New York, N.Y. 10016

10 9 8 7 6 5 4 3 2 1

Distributed in Canada by Sterling
Publishingc/o Canadian Manda Group,
One Atlantic Avenue, Suite 105
Toronto, Ontario, Canada M6K 3E7
Distributed in Australia by Capricorn
Link (Australia) Pty Ltd
P O. Box 6651, Baulkham Hills, Business
Centre, NSW 2153, Australia

Designed for Godsfield Press by
THE BRIDGEWATER BOOK COMPANY

Picture research Liz Moore
Design Glyn Bridgewater
Illustration: Joan Baker, Julian Baker
Photography: Ian Parsons

Printed and bound in Hong Kong

ISBN 0–8069–9855-5

Library of Congress Cataloging-in-Publication Dat
Craze, Richard, 1950-
  Fung shui made easy : an introduction to the basics of
the ancient art of feng shui / Richard Craze.
     p.   cm.
  Includes index.
  ISBN 0-8069-9855-5
  1. Feng-shui.   I. Title.
BF1779.F4C74   1999
133.3'337--dc21
                                    99-20804
                                    CIP

*ACKNOWLEDGMENTS
The publishers wish to thank the following for
the use of pictures:*
Arcaid/Richard Bryant: 37a, 37b, 54,
55b 57, 58, 60, 64, 66, 68, 70, 72.
Bridgeman Art Library: 6, 11b, 12br, 30
Images: 38, 39, 41, 55a, 78
Stockmarket: 7, 15b, 52, 53a
Stockmarket/Bill Miles: 36
Stockmarket/Bo Zaunders: 74

Contents

Introduction

Feng shui is an ancient Chinese art that seems to have no corresponding practice in the West. It involves deciding where to establish our homes and how to arrange our surroundings. This maximizes our potential as recipients of healthy, positive energy known as "ch'i" — cosmic life force. If the energy we

Above: **The art of feng shui has been practiced in China for centuries.**

receive is stagnant or unhealthy, it will affect us in a detrimental way, and we will suffer from bad luck, loss of money, poor-quality relationships, and ill-health. Once we correct the flow of the energy and make it healthy again, it will benefit us.

The practice of feng shui — which translates as "wind and water" — is based on sound commonsense, such as not building your home on the edge of a cliff, or directly above a marsh or swamp; not sitting at your desk with your back to a door (because it may make you feel unsettled); and having a home that is clean, uncluttered, and hygienic.

The study of feng shui can take many years and involve considerable effort. In *Feng Shui Made Easy*, important information has been distilled and presented in a clear and easy-to-understand format that will make your learning and understanding of this fascinating subject enjoyable and easy.

Right: **Good feng shui leads to personal happiness and success.**

History and Philosophy

The practice of feng shui is a skill that combines intuition, magic, interior design, commonsense, and an artistic drive. It can also be seen as a universal view that embraces heaven, earth, people, and energy. All these elements are connected by ch'i – the cosmic life force. By maximizing ch'i through feng shui, you can expand and improve your life in every aspect.

Chinese philosophy favors an approach to life in which everything is interconnected and nothing operates in isolation.

Above: **The yin and yang symbol represents harmony.**

The particular philosophy that is behind feng shui comes from the ancient Chinese religion of Taoism – the Way – which believes that energy is in constant flux, in and around us. Thus much of the philosophy behind feng shui is used, for example, in Chinese medicine.

Because the basic premise of Taoism is to live in the present,

Above: **In Chinese religion and philosophy, everything is interconnected by a constant flow of energy.**

Right: **To apply feng shui to a building or area, you first have to establish which way it faces.**

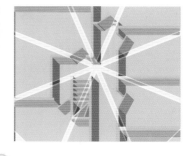

ollowers are encouraged to consider where they live and to ry and make life comfortable and evitalizing by maximizing a site's otential. This philosophy is also pplied to the home's interior.

Feng shui was widely racticed in modern-ay China until the ultural Revolution (1949). t is now making a popu-ar comeback and has been uccessfully introduced to he West.

Left: **As elements from the earth, the Chinese use crystals to bring ch'i into their homes.**

ight: **Four symbolic nimals – including e phoenix – feature in hinese religion. Each one elates to a compass point.**

The Three Types of Feng Shui

In China feng shui has traditionally been carried out by feng shui consultants called *feng shui hsien sheng* or Taoist priests. In the West professionals use feng shui and would practice one of three distinct schools of feng shui — lo p'an feng shui, pah kwa feng shui, and yin yang feng shui.

Below: **The geomancer's compass, called the "lo p'an," determines directions during feng shui.**

COMPASS OR LO P'AN FENG SHUI

This approach relies heavily on the use of a traditional feng shui compass, called a "lo p'an." This compass consists of up to 64 rings of information which a feng shui consultant uses to determine whether your house is "right" for you. Compass feng shui is a very traditional service in China, often provided for burial. The Chinese are very superstitious and believe that a person buried in a "wrong" place will return to haunt the living, so it is essential to align the grave correctly.

DIRECTIONAL OR PAH KWA FENG SHUI

This type of feng shui makes use of the direction your house faces to derive information, as well as dividing the house into eight areas, or enrichments – the "pah kwa" (sometimes spelled "bagua") – that govern every area of your life, including relationships, family, career, and health.

INTUITIVE OR YIN YANG FENG SHUI

This school of feng shui deals with the way energy flows in and around your home and how you fit in with that energy.

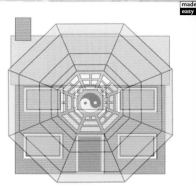

Above: **The home divides into eight areas or "enrichments" during the practice of pah kwa feng shui.**

Below: **This 16th-century Chinese painting shows the principle of feng shui applied to a traditional house.**

The Eight Remedies

Obviously, if ch'i energy is flowing badly or has become
unhealthy, it needs to be corrected. The eight remedies
are light, sound, color, life, movement, functional objects
(tools), stillness, and straight lines.

LIGHT

Light includes
mirrors to deflect
bad ch'i, lights to
brighten dull ch'i,
and candles to
warm cold ch'i.

COLOR

Anything from the color of the walls
to prints and paintings can be used
to stimulate the flow of ch'i.

SOUND

Sound includes
wind chimes to
stir up stagnant
ch'i, but can also,
in a modern
context, include
your CD player.

LIFE

Life: fish in tanks, plants, even a
sleeping cat will bring ch'i "to life."

MOVEMENT

Flags fluttering in the breeze, flowing water, smoke from incense, banners, and weather-vanes all help to stop ch'i from getting stale.

FUNCTIONAL OBJECTS

Functional objects include tools and electric devices, such as televisions, electric toasters, and even computers, all of which stir up dull ch'i.

STILLNESS

Statues, driftwood, crystals, ornaments, and objects can help slow down ch'i that is moving too fast.

STRAIGHT LINES

Scrolls, flutes, and swords hung along beams have been used traditionally to deflect ch'i when necessary.

Practical Feng Shui
Remedies

In addition to being a compass direction, each of the eight remedies has a particular enrichment area where it functions best. A remedy should be used either in the foyer or outside the house to counteract negative influences of disrupted ch'i.

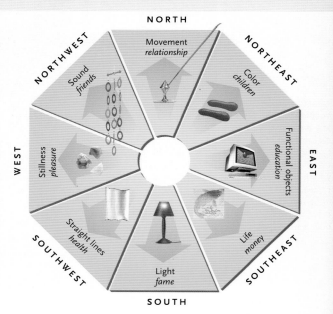

NORTH

Movement
relationship

NORTHEAST

Color
children

NORTHWEST

Sound
friends

EAST

Functional objects
education

WEST

Stillness
pleasure

SOUTHEAST

Life
money

SOUTHWEST

Straight lines
health

SOUTH

Light
fame

NORTHEAST EXAMPLE

Thus suppose your house faced northeast. Your front door would open directly out into the children area of life, and your enrichment area would be there. This would probably mean that your best way of earning a living or enjoying considerable reputation would be to link children with employment in some way — a nursery teacher, writer of children's books, or children's clothes designer, perhaps. If you suffer, in this area, from disrupted ch'i, try using a traditional remedy — such as color — to encourage ch'i. Paint your hall a brighter color, hang colored ribbons from your front door, use a painting of a bright color, paint the entire front door a bright color.

Left: **If your door opens to the northeast, it will affect the area of "children" in your life.**

NORTHEAST

Right: **A colorful front door encourages ch'i to enter your home and improve your life.**

The Four Compass Directions

The four compass directions are very important in feng shui. Each has its own characteristics, and it is important to know them — and in which direction your house faces — to understand what is happening to the energy reaching you.

WEST

West is an area of unpredictability, even danger. It contains warfare and strength, anger, suddenness, and potential violence. West's color is white, its element is metal, and its animals are dog, rooster, and monkey. Its season is the fall, and the ch'i from the west is unpredictable.

SOUTH

South represents luck, the summer, fame and fortune, happiness, light, joy, and hope. Its element is fire. The Chinese animals from astrology that favor the south are the goat, horse, and snake. Its season is the summer, and the ch'i that comes from the south is invigorating.

NORTH

North represents the hidden, the mysterious, coldness, sleep, ritual, nurture, and caring. North's color is black. Its element is water. Its animals are pig, rat, and ox. Its season is winter, and the ch'i from the north is protective and nurturing.

EAST

East is protective, cultured, wise, and represents new growth, kindness, and learning. The color of east is green; its element is wood, and its animals are tiger, hare, and dragon. Its season is spring, and the ch'i from the east is expansive and mature.

The Eight Life Areas

Our home, in traditional feng shui, is divided up into eight distinct areas of influence. Imagine your home to be in the shape of an octagon — each of these areas fits into one segment. How we arrange these segments and how the ch'i affects each of them is very important in pah kwa feng shui, since this octagon is the pah kwa.

THE EIGHT AREAS

Fame
3

Wealth
8

Wisdom and experience
1

Children and family
4

Relationships
9

Friends and new beginnings
2

Social activities
7

Health
6

You might notice that each of these areas is numbered. We will look at the reason for this when we learn about the "lo shu" – the Magic Square (see pages 22–23). Each of these eight areas of life is known as an "enrichment" as the eight different subjects all enrich our lives in different ways.

If any area is left to stagnate we will be poorer in sprit or materially, and according to feng shui philosophy, our aim is to be well rounded, complete individuals with everything in our lives moving in the right direction. We cannot afford to ignore any of these areas of life, as they all interconnect to benefit us.

RELATIONSHIPS

FRIENDS AND NEW BEGINNINGS

CHILDREN AND FAMILY

WISDOM AND EXPERIENCE

9

2

4

7

1

Around the center of your home are grouped the eight enrichments or life areas that govern every facet of our lives.

6

3

8

HEALTH

WEALTH

FAME

Practical Feng Shui
Overlaying the Pah Kwa

1 Draw up a basic house plan – draw an outline of each floor with the main rooms and main doorways to those rooms.

2 Make sure you know where south is and mark it on the side of your plan.

3 Now draw a rough octagonal shape over each ground plan that you have. If your house has more than one level, you will need a plan for each floor level. Divide the octagonal by connecting the eight sides to the middle.

THE PAH KWA AND THE GROUND FLOOR

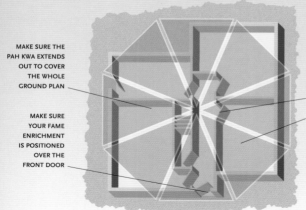

MAKE SURE THE PAH KWA EXTENDS OUT TO COVER THE WHOLE GROUND PLAN

MAKE SURE YOUR FAME ENRICHMENT IS POSITIONED OVER THE FRONT DOOR

YOU CAN CHECK THE COMPASS DIRECTION OF EACH ENRICHMENT AND SEE WHICH WAY IT FACES

IF THE FAME ENRICHMENT IS OVER THE FRONT DOOR, YOUR WEALTH ENRICHMENT IS ALWAYS TO THE RIGHT AS YOU ENTER

4 Write in the eight enrichments, starting with "fame" positioned over the front door for the ground floor. On upper floors, start with fame wherever the stairs arrive and work your way around the floor.

5 If you have a ground plan that indicates areas that are missing or look overly large, these will highlight problem areas in your life and should be improved with an appropriate remedy taken from pages 12-15 and in keeping with the particular enrichment.

6 You can do this overlaying the pah kwa for each floor if you wish, and then you can take it even farther and check the feng shui of each individual room. You can even do it for your desk, kitchen work surface, yard, office, or car.

THE PAH KWA AND THE FIRST FLOOR

MAKE SURE THE PAH KWA EXTENDS OUT OVER ALL THE PLAN, INCLUDING ANY EXTENSIONS

PLACE YOUR FAME ENRICH-MENT OVER THE STAIRS ON THE FIRST FLOOR TO SEE WHICH WAY EVERYTHING FACES

CHECK THE COMPASS DIRECTIONS OF ALL THE ROOMS UPSTAIRS

EXACTLY AS DOWNSTAIRS, YOUR WEALTH ENRICHMENT IS IMMEDIATELY TO THE RIGHT AS YOU GO UPSTAIRS

The Lo Shu Magic Square

We looked earlier at the octagon known as the pah kwa. Pulling the eight segments out into a square and numbering them as in the diagram creates a "lo shu" – a magic square. This is an important part of ancient feng shui and a basis for "walking the Nine Palaces" which we will look at on pages 44–45.

Above: A lo shu grid (to be placed over a floorplan) is always set up like this.

Each of the nine squares created has an enrichment, or life area, attached to it and can be overlaid onto a plan of your house to see where everything fits. Looking at the numbers, you might notice that any three added together horizontally, vertically, or diagonally total 15. This particular number is considered very lucky by the Chinese because it represents yin and yang as well as ch'i in Chinese calligraphy. The lo shu will also give you times of the day, the Chinese astrological animals, and the compass directions (see pages 16–17 and 42–43).

The lo shu gives us direction – 1 faces south and 9 faces north; 3 faces west and 7 east. 1 is also summer, 9 winter, 3 fall, and 7 spring. This also gives us the time: start at 1 for noon.

The center of the lo shu is numbered 5 and left blank. It represents jen hsin – the home's center, the heart of life, and traditionally a space to be filled by the occupant.

THE MAGIC SQUARE OVER A HOUSE PLAN

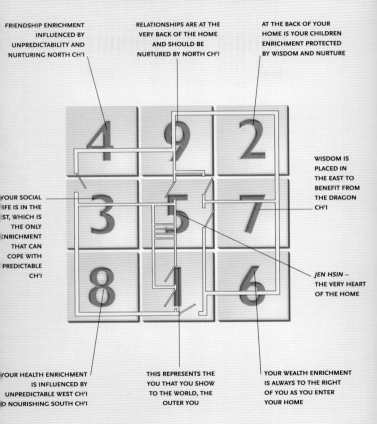

FRIENDSHIP ENRICHMENT
INFLUENCED BY
UNPREDICTABILITY AND
NURTURING NORTH CH'I

RELATIONSHIPS ARE AT THE
VERY BACK OF THE HOME
AND SHOULD BE
NURTURED BY NORTH CH'I

AT THE BACK OF YOUR
HOME IS YOUR CHILDREN
ENRICHMENT PROTECTED
BY WISDOM AND NURTURE

WISDOM IS
PLACED IN
THE EAST TO
BENEFIT FROM
THE DRAGON
CH'I

YOUR SOCIAL
LIFE IS IN THE
EAST, WHICH IS
THE ONLY
ENRICHMENT
THAT CAN
COPE WITH
PREDICTABLE
CH'I

JEN HSIN –
THE VERY HEART
OF THE HOME

YOUR HEALTH ENRICHMENT
IS INFLUENCED BY
UNPREDICTABLE WEST CH'I
AND NOURISHING SOUTH CH'I

THIS REPRESENTS THE
YOU THAT YOU SHOW
TO THE WORLD, THE
OUTER YOU

YOUR WEALTH ENRICHMENT
IS ALWAYS TO THE RIGHT
OF YOU AS YOU ENTER
YOUR HOME

The Five Elements

> **A fundamental part of feng shui is the Five Element Theory. This suggests that everything in the universe is formed by a combination of five basic components — water, fire, wood, earth, and metal.**

The uniqueness of everything depends on the proportions of these five elements — and that includes us. We are considered to be predominately one of these five elements, depending on the year in which we were born. To work out which element most closely represents you, look at the last number of the year of your birth.

FINDING YOUR ELEMENT

last number in birth year	yin/yang	element
0	yang	metal
1	yin	metal
2	yang	water
3	yin	water
4	yang	wood
5	yin	wood
6	yang	fire
7	yin	fire
8	yang	earth
9	yin	earth

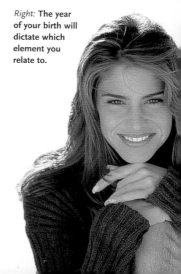

Right: **The year of your birth will dictate which element you relate to.**

EARTH

The five elements,
fundamental to
feng shui, all
interconnect and
affect each other.

FIRE

METAL

WOOD

WATER

Practical Feng Shui
Element Characteristics

Fire types like to live in south-facing homes and should use reds and oranges as main colors in decoration and dress; water types should face north and use dark blues and black; earth types should live in centrally placed homes and use yellows and ocher; wood types should face east and use green; metal types should face west and use white, silver, and gray.

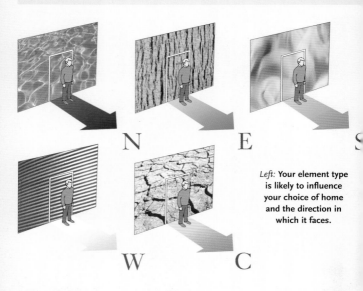

N   E   S

W   C

Left: **Your element type is likely to influence your choice of home and the direction in which it faces.**

Water: *the Thinker,* loves knowledge and intellectual pursuits, hates to be vulnerable, and should avoid cold

Wood: *the Explorer,* loves to be busy and purposeful, hates to lose, and should avoid windy places

Fire: *the Adventurer,* loves change, hates boredom, and should avoid heat

Earth: *the Diplomat* loves people and to be of use, hates being ignored, should avoid damp

Metal: *the Catalyst,* loves to be precise and controlling, hates disorder and clutter, and should avoid dryness

The Five Helpers and the Five Hinderers

Obviously if you are one element type and your partner or children are another type or types, there will be times when you get along and times when you don't. Each of the elements has a cycle whereby it is said to help or hinder the other elements. These cycles are shown on the diagram opposite.

- **Earth** helps metal, is helped by fire, hinders water, is hindered by wood

- **Fire** helps earth, is helped by wood, hinders metal, is hindered by water

- **Water** helps wood, is helped by metal, hinders fire, is hindered by earth

- **Metal** helps water, is helped by earth, hinders wood, is hindered by fire

- **Wood** helps fire, is helped by water, hinders earth, is hindered by metal

Above: **Parenting may sometimes be tested if your child is an element type that hinders your own.**

This diagram explains the relationships between all five elements.

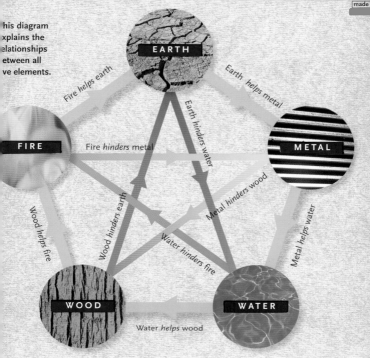

EARTH

Fire *helps* earth

Earth *helps* metal

Earth hinders water

METAL

FIRE

Fire *hinders* metal

Metal hinders wood

Metal *helps* water

Wood *hinders* earth

Water hinders fire

Wood *helps* fire

WOOD

WATER

Water *helps* wood

Think of this in terms of practical uses for these elements – for instance, metal could be an ax or a bucket. As an axe it would be unhelpful to wood, but as a bucket it would be helpful to water. Water helps wood by making it grow but in turn hinders fire by putting it out. Earth hinders water by blocking its flow.

Yin and Yang

In Taoist philosophy everything in the universe is either yin or yang — or a combination of both. It is believed that, from the Great Cosmos, energy was generated that gave birth to the heavens — yang — and the earth — yin. Ch'i flows from yang to yin and from yin to yang. The universe is in a state of constant change as that energy is altered from matter — yin — to spirit — yang — and back again.

Above: **The yin and yang symbol is at the center of this carving from the Chengdu Temple in China.**

As feng shui concerns energy management, it is important to know how yang and yin operate. They shouldn't be seen as opposites, although they do have certain characteristics that might be taken that way: the yang principle is known as the male principle, whereas the yin is the female. However, nothing is ever entirely one or the other. The yin/yang symbol reflects this — in the white of the yang is the dot of dark yin, and in the black of the yin is the white dot of yang.

THE ATTRIBUTES GIVEN TO YIN AND YANG

Yin	Yang		Yin	Yang
inner	outer	receptive	creative
north	south	dark	light
down	up	night	day
matter	spirit	cold	heat
earth	sky	soft	hard
negative	positive	wet	dry
passive	active	winter	summer
female	male	shadow	sunshine

The Eight Types of Ch'i

From each of the eight compass directions, the ch'i that flows — and affects us when it reaches us — has a different quality. It can also deteriorate into different types of "sha" — unhealthy or negative ch'i. The eight different types of sha all cause different problems.

THE EFFECTS OF CH'I

South	*vigorous ch'i* degrades to accelerating sha, which causes feelings of exhaustion
North	*nurturing ch'i* degrades to lingering sha, which causes feelings of lethargy
East	*growing ch'i* degrades to overpowering sha, which causes feelings of egotism and vanity
West	*changeable ch'i* degrades to dangerous sha, which causes rash action
Southeast	*creative ch'i* degrades to provoking sha, which causes feelings of irritability and headaches
Southwest	*soothing ch'i* degrades to disruptive sha, which causes feelings of anger
Northeast	*flourishing ch'i* degrades to stagnating sha, which causes ill-health
Northwest	*expansive ch'i* degrades to unpredictable sha, which causes restlessness

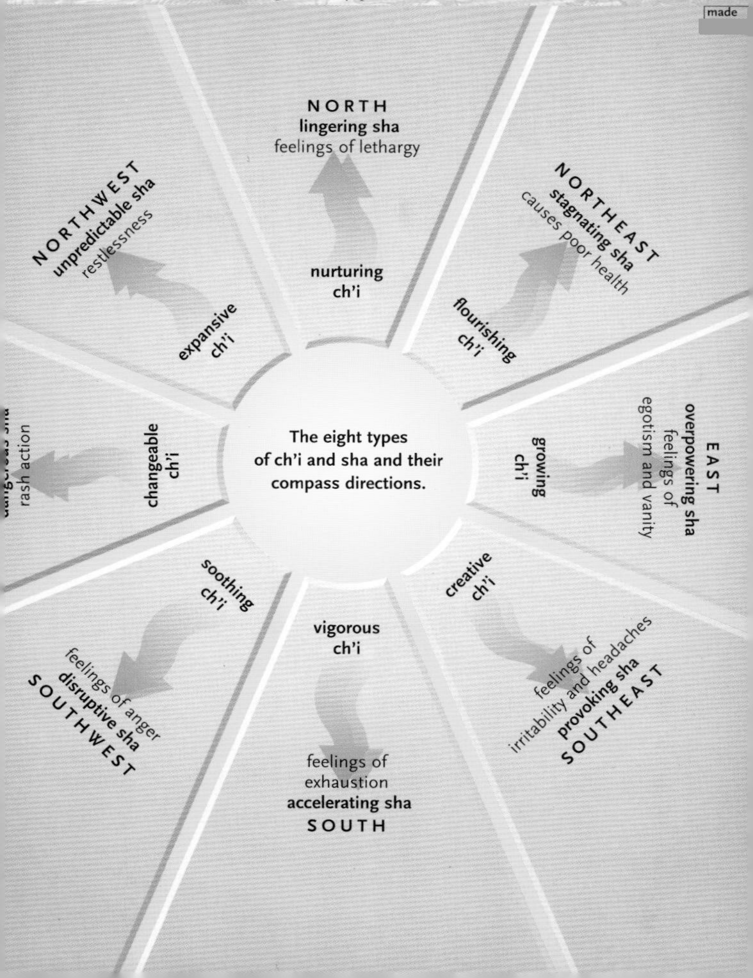

NORTH
lingering sha
feelings of lethargy

NORTHWEST
unpredictable sha
restlessness

NORTHEAST
stagnating sha
causes poor health

nurturing ch'i

expansive ch'i

flourishing ch'i

rash action

changeable ch'i

The eight types of ch'i and sha and their compass directions.

growing ch'i

EAST
overpowering sha
feelings of egotism and vanity

soothing ch'i

creative ch'i

feelings of anger
disruptive sha
SOUTHWEST

vigorous ch'i

feelings of irritability and headaches
provoking sha
SOUTHEAST

feelings of exhaustion
accelerating sha
SOUTH

Practical Feng Shui
The Eight Types of Ch'i

We need to know how each of the eight types of ch'i affects
us, as our house or office – or even backyard – is capable
of facing in any one of eight different directions. Thus if
our front door opens to the southwest, the ch'i coming from
that direction will affect us completely differently than if our
home faced northeast.

Each direction brings ch'i with its own particular quality, and if our front door opens in that direction, that quality – and of course its negative attributes if the ch'i has been allowed to stagnate become blocked, or encouraged flow too quickly – will manifest every way in our lives. This negativity should be resolved.

1	Fame	South	Vigorous
2	Friendships	Northwest	Expansive
3	Wisdom	East	Growing
4	Children	Northeast	Flourishing
5	Relationships	North	Nurturing
6	Health	Southwest	Soothing
7	Social	West	Changeable
8	Wealth	Southeast	Creative

Left: **Each
compass
direction brings
ch'i that will
affect certain
areas of our lives**

Above: **The Green Dragon offers protection if your front door faces east.**

You can see from the chart on the left that if your front door opens into the east, you draw from the strength of wisdom and experience, you benefit from growing ch'i, and you are under the protection of the Green Dragon (see page 42). If you face west, you enjoy changeable circumstances, which mainly affect your social life – you do battle with the White Tiger.

Rules of Ch'i

The flow of energy is dependent on a number of things, and the way it flows varies, too. Ch'i has certain likes and dislikes, and if we want it to flow well, we are advised to prepare the groundwork first. If we don't, the ch'i can stagnate, become too fast, become too dull or lethargic, or simply turn into sha, which brings ill-health and bad luck.

Ch'i likes to flow along clear and harmonious routes. This means no clutter and no obstructions. It also likes neatness, cleanliness, order, curves, and balance. If your home needs redecorating, do it, or the ch'i will also be in need of attention. If your home is cluttered and messy, clear it up, or the ch'i will become confused. If your home is dark and badly lit, the ch'i will be stale and listless. Ch'i favors hidden corners, but it doesn't like to stagnate there. Corners are fine as long as the ch'i can circulate well.

Above: **A cluttered home is not conducive to free-flowing ch'i. Ch'i prefers plenty of space so it can move around the house with ease.**

Right: **This building both encourages and hinders ch'i.**

CH'I LIKES CURVES BECAUSE THEY DO NOT HINDER ITS PROGRESS

THIS TREE BLOCKS CH'I FROM ENTERING THE BUILDING

Below: **This building is ideal for the flow of ch'i because it is uncluttered and open.**

Practical Feng Shui
Being Ch'i

Go outside your house. Stand with your back to the front door. This is an important exercise as it shows you exactly what influences your house and your life are directly under.

What can you see? Is it a view you like? Is it pleasant? Is there anything you would change? Do you look out on a factory, police station, cemetery, industrial site, prison, or army barracks? Any of these would, according to traditional feng shui practitioners, affect you badly. Depending on your house's direction, you will need a remedy to counteract any negative energy coming toward

Above: **Overly quiet and uniform suburban streets can cause lethargy.**

Above: **A streetlight and road directly outside your front door will block ch'i from entering.**

ou from such locations. If, on the ther hand, you look out on open reen fields, woods, and a stream, ou have, traditionally, a good ocation and should enjoy it.

Watch out for streetlights irectly in front of your house or rees too close to your windows – hey stop the ch'i from entering – oads aimed directly at your ouse, hills too large or imposing lirectly in front of your main loor, unpleasant or disruptive eighbors, too much activity such

as being opposite a school or shopping center (these can make you feel irritable and rushed), too little activity such as a completely dead landscape with no wildlife or activity, or a too-quiet suburban street (these can make you feel lethargic and unstimulated).

Do this exercise for each of the eight compass directions and see what influences each of the eight enrichments is coming under and what changes in the way of remedies you need to make.

Above: **Trees outside your windows are a bad idea because they are an obstacle to ch'i.**

Above: **Potentially this house has good ch'i, but it is hindered by the plant blocking the door.**

The Four Seasons

The four seasons are important since feng shui is as much about living in harmony with nature and the environment as it is about energy management. It is important to know how the four seasons relate to the five elements and the four compass directions (see pages 16–17 and 24–25).

If you're wondering where Earth fits in, it is right in the center, surrounded by the other four elements on all four sides. You can see how all this fits together by imagining spring, for instance.

Spring is a time of new growth – hence wood and green. Winter, on the other hand, is cold, north, black, and water.

Above: Winter, spring, summer, and fall all affect the feng shui of your home.

EASON	DIRECTION/COLOR	ANIMAL	ELEMENT
ummer	South/Red	Phoenix	Fire
utumn	West/White	White Tiger	Metal
Spring	East/Green	Dragon	Wood
Winter	North/Black	Tortoise	Water

The Four Symbolic Animals

Each of the four main compass directions is ruled by a symbolic animal. These magical animals appear constantly throughout Chinese art and culture, and represent directions, colors, seasons, and enrichments.

West: the tiger, called Wu, the White Tiger. West is an area of unpredictability, even danger. It contains warfare and strength, the fall, anger, suddenness, and potential violence.

South: the phoenix, known as the Red Bird of the South. The phoenix is called Feng Huang (it can also be a pheasant, rooster, or any bright bird) and represents luck, the summer, fame and fortune, happiness, light, joy, and hope.

North: the tortoise, named Yuan Wu, the Black Tortoise (can also be a coiled snake, a turtle, and even smoke). North represents the hidden, the mysterious, winter, sleep, ritual, nurture, and caring.

East: the dragon, known as Wen, the Green Dragon (which can sometimes be gold but is always a dragon). East is protective, cultured, wise, spring, kindness, and learning.

The Nine Palaces and The Nine Questions

When you want to check the feng shui of your home, your yard, or your business, the way to do it is to walk the Nine Palaces. This means walking into each of the eight enrichments in the same order as they are numbered on this page. The center of your home is numbered 5 — *jen hsin* — which represents the heart of the home.

Above: The nine squares of the lo shu are known as the Nine Palaces.

In each enrichment you should stop for a while and ask yourself the Nine Questions about this area. These questions are:

- How does it look?

- How does it feel?

- Is the furniture appropriate?

- Am I happy with the decor?

- What do I use this area for and is it appropriate?

- What would I change?

- What would I improve?

- What do I like?

- What don't I like?

WHAT DO I USE
THIS AREA FOR
AND IS IT
APPROPRIATE?

HOW DOES IT LOOK?
WHAT WOULD I
CHANGE? WHAT
WOULD I IMPROVE?

WHAT DO I USE THIS
AREA FOR? WHAT DO
I LIKE? WHAT DON'T
I LIKE?

HOW DOES
IT FEEL? IS THE
FURNITURE
APPROPRIATE?

Traditionally, all of these questions would have been asked of you by your feng shui consultant or Taoist priest, who did the same job), but you can ask them

Above: **Always ask yourself the Nine Questions as you enter a new room.**

of yourself. When you have established answers to all your questions, think about how you could resolve them and implement appropriate changes.

The Eight House Directions

When you open the front door, or main entrance, to your home, you will be facing in one of eight compass directions. This "sets" the house direction, and each compass point has a different meaning.

Above: An adventurer is likely to have a front door facing out to the east. These people belong to the great outdoors and are restless in any other environment.

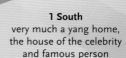

1 South
very much a yang home,
the house of the celebrity
and famous person

2 Southeast
the home of the entrepreneur
and the business person

3 East
a yang house of someone
who likes exploring the world

6 Northeast
the house of those involved in
research and science, combining
wisdom with authority and teaching

4 Southwest
house of someone who uses their
ing, nurturing side to help others,
the house of the healer

7 Northwest
the house of someone who looks
out for others – care workers and
police officers favor this direction

5 North
he home of the great lover, ideal
r generating new relationships, or
nurturing a good long-term one

8 West
the house of the social entertainer,
the food lover, the raconteur, and the
pleasure seeker

The Eight Trigrams

In China, each of the eight house directions has traditionally been given a trigram. This is made by combining the two yin/yang lines. Each of these eight trigrams has certain qualities ascribed to it.

Right: **People, heaven and the earth all appear in the trigrams — heaven resides in the highest position, people are in the middle, and the earth is in the lowest position.**

Trigram	Chinese Title	Western Title	Direction	Season	Aspect
Ch'ien	The Creative	Heaven	South	Summer	Energy
Tui	The Lake	Pleasure	Southeast	Early Summer	Joy
Li	The Fire	Clinging	East	Spring	Intelligence
Chen	The Thunder	Arousing	Northeast	Early Spring	Excitement
K'un	The Receptive	Creation	North	Winter	Nourishment
Ken	The Mountain	Stillness	Northwest	Early Winter	Calmness
K'an	The Moon	Water	West	Fall	Unpredictable
H'sun	The Wind	Gentleness	Southwest	Early Fall	Movement

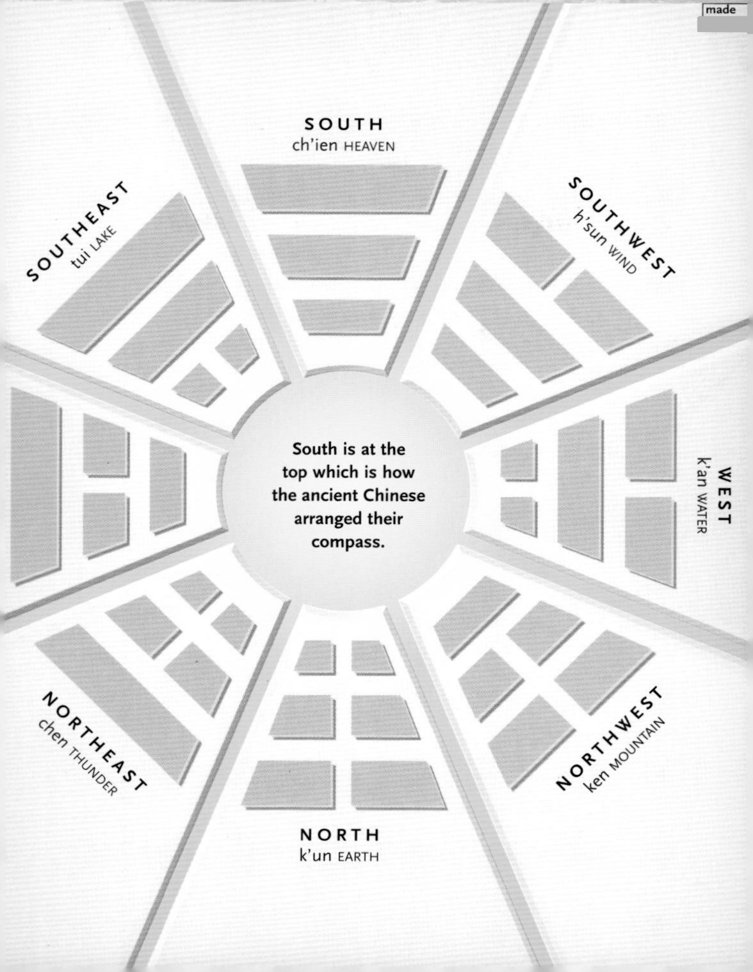

SOUTH
ch'ien HEAVEN

SOUTHEAST
tui LAKE

SOUTHWEST
h'sun WIND

WEST
k'an WATER

South is at the
top which is how
the ancient Chinese
arranged their
compass.

NORTHEAST
chen THUNDER

NORTHWEST
ken MOUNTAIN

NORTH
k'un EARTH

The *I Ching*

This oracle was originally written to help farmers plant crops, as it gave seasons, weather conditions, and the best locations for creating fields. Today, it is better known as a fortune-telling device. The 64 hexagrams are important as they combine the eight house directions with the eight enrichments to arrive at 64 different readings for home arrangements. The *I Ching* can be used as a seasonal method of rearranging or adjusting your furniture, furnishings, and decor.

With a copy of the *I Ching* and knowledge of your house direction and where the eight enrichments fall, you can read any of the 64 readings in the *I Ching* and apply them to your home.

The *I Ching* may well be the oldest book on the planet. It is certainly the oldest book in printed form – and one that is still in use today. It dates originally back to the third millennium B.C. and is accredited to Fu His, who may

have been a legendary ruler of China during that time.

Feng shui and the *I Ching* are closely connected, and a study of one will invariably lead to a study of the other.

Right: **The *I Ching* is among the oldest manuscripts and gives 64 readings that may be applied to your home.**

made

By combining feng shui
with readings from the *I Ching*
you can discover how best to
organize your home.

Rules of Sha

**Sha is unhealthy ch'i, and it brings us ill-health and bad luck.
Sha likes to travel along fast, straight paths where it can
accelerate and then drive through you at great speed. The
difference between sha and ch'i is the same as the difference
between a straight canal and a gentle meandering river. Sha is
the canal and ch'i is the river. One will be devoid of life and
interest and the other will attract life and beauty.**

Sha likes clutter, disorder, chaos, and confusion. It also likes mess, dirt, badly decorated rooms, decay, and being trapped. If you want to attract sha instead of ch'i, just allow your home to be dark and confused, messy, and un-hygienic. Of course, if you want good healthy ch'i you have to do some work – decorating, cleaning straightening, and restoring order

Sha will cause bad luck, poor health, troubled relationships naughty, noisy children, loss of job or money, lack of success – and a general feeling of depression and lethargy. A good strong blast o clean ch'i will reverse all that.

Above: Ch'i can be likened to a meandering river, preferring corners to straight lines.

Right: The design of this house encourages ch'i because straight edges are balanced by a curving staircase.

CURVES
ENCOURAGE CH'I

Left: Although this river looks beautiful, sha would travel easily along its straight banks.

The Feng Shui of Famous Buildings

Looking at an aerial view of the White House, you would see three roads converging on it. In feng shui this is known as "arrowhead killing ch'i," and it makes any occupant of a house faced with this configuration feel restless, aggressive, and belligerent.

The Taj Mahal, built in India in the seventeenth century, has a similar road pointing straight to it, but since it is deflected by the large pool of water in front of the mausoleum, any harmful sha is absorbed, causing a powerful sense of peace and tranquility

Below: **Any sha is absorbed by the pool of water before the Taj Mahal.**

made
easy

Left: **The traffic circle in front of Britain's Buckingham Palace does not favor the monarchy.**

Below: **The Hong Kong and Shanghai Bank was designed using feng shui principles.**

Buckingham Palace, the home of the current monarch in Great Britain, has a traffic circle built directly in front of it. This causes a loss of face in Chinese terms, which can be read as signifying a reduction in the popular support for the monarchy.

Today feng shui has a valid place in modern building design, and feng shui principles have influenced the design of some important sites, like the Bank of China and the Hong Kong and Shanghai Bank in Hong Kong.

The Hyatt Hotel in Singapore has reported considerable upturn in business since it adapted its building to improve the feng shui.

Famous People who use Feng Shui

Many successful and famous people have incorporated feng shui principles into their own homes. They include Richard Branson, the late Diana, Princess of Wales, Donald Trump, Michael Caine, Anita Roddick, and Boy George.

In the United Kingdom the house building firm, Wimpey Homes, has issued a 12-page "beginner's guide to feng shui" for prospective purchasers of new homes. Wimpey reports great interest in the feng shui of its Britannia Village development, in the Docklands of London, from Japanese customers.

Wimpey Homes are not alone. Other companies that practice feng shui principles in their businesses include Marks and Spencer, Virgin Atlantic, the Ritz hotel chain, and the Orange mobile-phone network.

Another company in the United Kingdom embracing this ancient art for interiors is the home-improvements chain, B&Q Warehouse. When it opened it first B&Q in the Far East, in Tai wan, the General Manager, Davi Inglis, became intrigued: "At firs I thought it was just rather amus ing, but when I saw how deepl the Taiwanese believed in it, an how strictly they made feng shu principles a way of life, I began t read more about it and becam more deeply interested myself. This enthusiasm for feng shui spreading across the world.

Right: **The design this modern bedroom ha obvious traditional orient influences, with its clea and uncluttered loo**

The Feng Shui Bedroom

There are two important rules to consider when checking the feng shui of your bedroom: there should be no beams above the bed, and the bed should not be directly opposite the door.

If you have beams and cannot rearrange your bedroom by moving the bed away, hanging fabric from the beams will interrupt the accelerated flow of ch'i, preventing it from bringing poor health.

Ideally, you should position the bed to give a good vantage point so that you see anyone coming into the room before they see you. The Chinese believe that a dead person is always carried out feet first from the bedroom, so don't have your feet directly opposite the door!

Bedrooms should be as light and uncluttered as possible so that the ch'i can restore us while we are asleep. The bed should be as high as possible off the floor and as comfortable, decadent, and luxurious as you like.

A bedroom only needs a bed in it – you shouldn't really be using it as an office or study as well.

Right: **This peaceful feng shui bedroom is softly lit and sparsely furnished.**

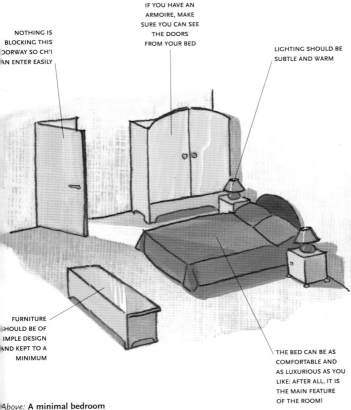

NOTHING IS
BLOCKING THIS
DOORWAY SO CH'I
CAN ENTER EASILY

IF YOU HAVE AN
ARMOIRE, MAKE
SURE YOU CAN SEE
THE DOORS
FROM YOUR BED

LIGHTING SHOULD BE
SUBTLE AND WARM

FURNITURE
SHOULD BE OF
SIMPLE DESIGN
AND KEPT TO A
MINIMUM

THE BED CAN BE AS
COMFORTABLE AND
AS LUXURIOUS AS YOU
LIKE: AFTER ALL, IT IS
THE MAIN FEATURE
OF THE ROOM!

Above: A minimal bedroom
is a feng shui bedroom.

The Feng Shui Bathroom

The very worst thing, according to traditional feng shui principles, is to have the toilet directly opposite the door. The Chinese, like many oriental races, are extremely private and would not consider being seen sitting on the john to be a good thing.

The toilet seat should never b left up. If the toilet can be see from the door, you should con sider screening it.

The bathroom should be kep clean and hygienic – avoid clutte and messy areas in this room i you can, as the ch'i will not onl stagnate here but rapidly decay allowing damp and condensatio to set in.

Bathrooms are yin rooms and need to be plainly decorated and any furnishings kept very simple Mirrors in bathrooms should no

Left: **Work out which enrichment area your bathroom is in and whether it is the cause of any problems; a lot of ch'i disappears with used water.**

made

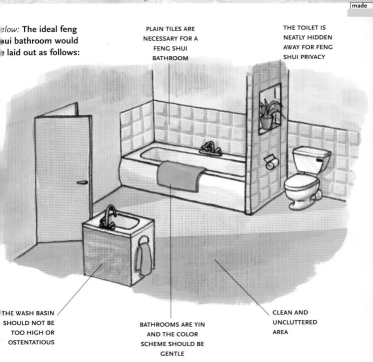

Below: **The ideal feng shui bathroom would be laid out as follows:**

PLAIN TILES ARE NECESSARY FOR A FENG SHUI BATHROOM

THE TOILET IS NEATLY HIDDEN AWAY FOR FENG SHUI PRIVACY

THE WASH BASIN SHOULD NOT BE TOO HIGH OR OSTENTATIOUS

BATHROOMS ARE YIN AND THE COLOR SCHEME SHOULD BE GENTLE

CLEAN AND UNCLUTTERED AREA

be in front of windows, nor should they be too high or low.

See which enrichment your bathroom falls into – this may give you a clue to any problem areas in your life. It may be that any energy is being flushed away, or drained out with the bath water, and you'll need to keep that toilet seat down.

The Feng Shui Kitchen

This should be the very heart of the home and can benefit more than any other room from good feng shui. Kitchens are not necessarily rooms to entertain in so you can design them in a particularly indulgent way — they are for you to work in happily and they should suit you.

If you are very tall, raise all your work surfaces — and do the opposite if you are small. Nobody should be able to walk behind you without your seeing them, so lots of mirrors are important. Anything not being used, such as blenders, mixers, and food processors should be put away when not in use as they are powerful mechanical device remedies. Remember that in kitchens certain elements work in opposition — don't have fire (the stove) next to water (the refrigerator), or wood (the work surfaces perhaps) next to metal (the knives — they should always be stored away). This is because water and fire, wood and metal, are directly opposite each other on the compass.

Left: **The neat and simple design of this modern kitchen gives good feng shui and a fashionable look.**

made

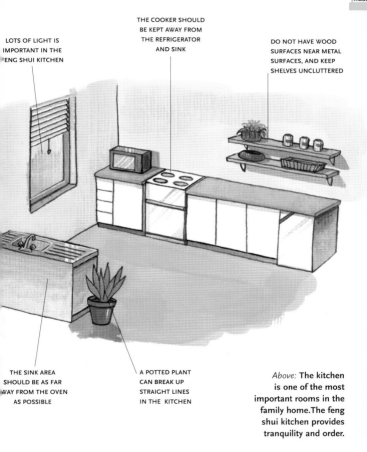

THE COOKER SHOULD
BE KEPT AWAY FROM
THE REFRIGERATOR
AND SINK

LOTS OF LIGHT IS
IMPORTANT IN THE
FENG SHUI KITCHEN

DO NOT HAVE WOOD
SURFACES NEAR METAL
SURFACES, AND KEEP
SHELVES UNCLUTTERED

THE SINK AREA
SHOULD BE AS FAR
AWAY FROM THE OVEN
AS POSSIBLE

A POTTED PLANT
CAN BREAK UP
STRAIGHT LINES
IN THE KITCHEN

Above: **The kitchen
is one of the most
important rooms in the
family home. The feng
shui kitchen provides
tranquility and order.**

The Feng Shui Study

If you use a study at home, there are a few rules you can apply. If your study is used for work — for making money — try to position it in the wealth enrichment.

This means getting it as close as possible to the left-hand corner of your home, next to the front door and facing out. Thus when you come home, your study would be in the room immediately on your right as you open the front door.

Don't sit with your back to the door of your study; this can cause restlessness and even nervousness. Turn the desk around so you are facing the door and can see anyone about to come in. Try not to have your computer screen placed directly underneath a window so that you are looking out of the window at the same time as at the screen. If possible, position the window behind you.

Above: **The study is a place for contemplation as well as business. To maximize enrichment from your study, try to locate it as near as possible to the front door.**

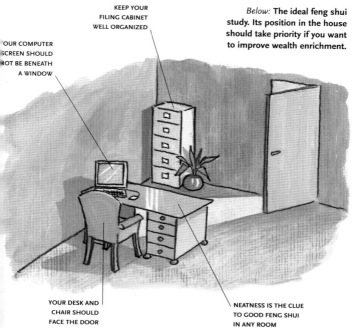

KEEP YOUR
FILING CABINET
WELL ORGANIZED

Below: The ideal feng shui
study. Its position in the house
should take priority if you want
to improve wealth enrichment.

YOUR COMPUTER
SCREEN SHOULD
NOT BE BENEATH
A WINDOW

YOUR DESK AND
CHAIR SHOULD
FACE THE DOOR

NEATNESS IS THE CLUE
TO GOOD FENG SHUI
IN ANY ROOM

Keep clutter to a minimum, including inside your filing cabinet. Throw papers away after three months unless you really need them. Be ruthless – it counts up all too quickly.

If you use a computer, run a screensaver for times when you're not using it. Computers are powerful remedies, and a little movement will ease their potential for exciting ch'i too much.

The Feng Shui Living Room

In times past we centered our living room around an open fire — a good remedy as it incorporates movement, color, light, and even sound. Today, the tendency is to focus on the television set, which is a powerful mechanical remedy and its color, light, and sound are all "dead." Ideally, keep the television hidden unless it is needed, and go back to an open fire.

Left: **This light, spacious living room employs lots of feng shui principles to create a relaxed atmosphere.**

enrichment the living room falls in and also its compass direction. Use the four colors of the four directions: if the living room is in the north, add lots of red to warm it up. If it is in the south, add lots of blue to cool it down. If it is in the east, add lots of white to slow it down. If it is in the west, add lots of green to calm it down.

Arrange your furniture into an octagon if you can, so that sofas cut across corners rather than being in straight lines. Make the lighting soft and subtle — with no bare light bulbs. Check which

If you have a dining area, or the living room opens onto the kitchen, you should try to screen it off from the living area. You might be able to use a trellis with climbing plants. Watch out for corners jutting into the room – these should be rounded off with plants. Try to keep the room as uncluttered as possible so the ch'i can circulate evenly.

If you have any mirrors in the living room, make sure that they don't "behead" you when you look in them. They should be angled so that you can see yourself clearly.

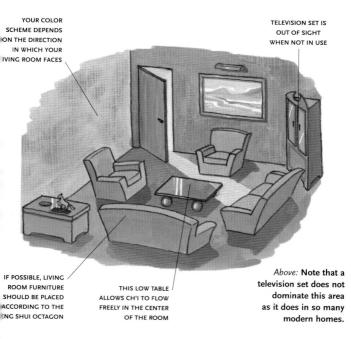

YOUR COLOR SCHEME DEPENDS ON THE DIRECTION IN WHICH YOUR LIVING ROOM FACES

TELEVISION SET IS OUT OF SIGHT WHEN NOT IN USE

IF POSSIBLE, LIVING ROOM FURNITURE SHOULD BE PLACED ACCORDING TO THE FENG SHUI OCTAGON

THIS LOW TABLE ALLOWS CH'I TO FLOW FREELY IN THE CENTER OF THE ROOM

Above: **Note that a television set does not dominate this area as it does in so many modern homes.**

The Feng Shui Dining Room

Hopefully, your dining room will fall in the social activity enrichment and be on the right-hand side of your home when you are facing the front door. Dining rooms are for entertaining guests as well as eating as a family, and they should be spacious, warm, and comfortable and be near to the kitchen so the food arrives hot.

Dining rooms shouldn't have to double up as studies or tool sheds, so keep the clutter out and use this room as it was intended. Arrange that furniture so as many guests as possible can see the door . Ideally the furniture should follow an octagon shape as far as possible.

Make sure there is plenty of room to open the door and walk around the table and chairs without feeling cramped. If you can't do this, you need a smaller table. Mirrors will help the room to feel larger – they should be placed so they reflect the food on the table.

Left: **The feng shui dining room is separate from the living area and is ideal for peaceful meals.**

ANY MIRRORS IN
THE ROOM SHOULD
REFLECT FOOD
ON THE TABLE

Below: **The feng shui dining room is exclusively for eating together.**

YOU SHOULD BE ABLE
TO EXIT EASILY TO THE
NEARBY KITCHEN

AS MANY OF YOUR
GUESTS AND FAMILY
AS POSSIBLE SHOULD
BE ABLE TO SEE
THE DOOR

Feng Shui Halls and Corridors

Long corridors can funnel ch'i too quickly, but this problem can be remedied — break them up with hanging banners, wind chimes, or flags. Small, foreshortened corridors can be expanded with a mirror on the end wall, on either of the side walls, or even on the ceiling.

Landings, hopefully, should be light and airy. If they aren't, try leaving a suitable landing door open and reflect a pleasant view with a strategically placed mirror.

The wider and brighter your corridors and landings are, the better. Use mirrors to make them seem wider if necessary, and keep some of the doors that lead off them open to let in more light and give a greater feeling of space. Try to avoid dark corridors since sha likes to collect there and make you feel unsettled. If it is difficult to direct natural light into the space, brighten up the corridor with electric lights.

Above: This landing is well lit and spacious, and should encourage ch'i to flow freely.

IF YOU HAVE SMALL
WINDOWS, DON'T
HESITATE TO USE
ELECTRIC LIGHTING

IF A HALL OR CORRIDOR
IS CRAMPED, USE
MIRRORS TO CREATE A
SPACIOUS EFFECT

POTTED PLANTS CAN
BE USED TO BREAK UP
STRAIGHT LINES

AVOID DARK COLORS
IN YOUR HALL, SINCE
THEY COLLECT SHA

Above: **The feng shui
hall is as light and
airy as possible.**

Feng Shui Stairs

Stairways allow the ch'i to flow up to the upper floors and also down away from them. If the stairs are too close to the front door, the ch'i will flow down and straight out.

If ch'i can flow too freely, the upstairs rooms will feel drained and empty. Breaking up the flow of ch'i with a wind chime or even a well-placed plant could be beneficial here.

Above: **Staircases are crucial in a feng shui home, as they channel ch'i through the house.**

Stairs with bends in them can help the ch'i to flow well, as ch'i likes to curve and meander. However, you may find that if the bend is too sharp or even severe, the ch'i will not be able to turn properly. This can be remedied by using a small mirror on the wall.

Spiral staircases are a problem – they are so nice and curvy, the ch'i likes to disappear too quickly down them. Try placing a small mirror, face up, underneath the stairs to reflect some of the ch'i back upstairs.

The trick with stairs is to stand at the top and then at the bottom and imagine you are the ch'i. Ask yourself where you would flow, how quickly you would move, what you would encounter, and what would help you.

Below: **The stairway has to be carefully considered so that it neither blocks ch'i, or encourages it to flow too quickly through the home.**

THE DOORWAY SHOULD NOT BE TOO CLOSE TO THE STAIRS

STAIRCASES WITH BENDS IN THEM AID THE FLOW OF CH'I

POTTED PLANTS SLOW DOWN THE FLOW OF CH'I THROUGH THE HOUSE

A NEAT UNCLUTTERED AREA AROUND THE BASE OF THE STAIRS IS PREFERABLE

Feng Shui Doorways

Doors and windows should open in to allow the ch'i free access. If they open out, put a small mirror onto the wall they face when open. Doors should not open onto a solid wall or the ch'i will be blocked. There should not be any furniture blocking easy access into the room.

Above: **Doors and windows should open in to give ch'i easy access into the home.**

Doors should open and close with ease. If you have to push or pull hard to close a door, think what the ch'i has to do to pass through it. Oil the hinges and allow easy access. Squeaky doors should be treated in the same way.

Doors should be in proportion to the room size – too large, and they allow any ch'i to escape; too small, and they restrict the ch'i from entering. You need to slow down or encourage the ch'i respectively by using suitable remedies. If the door is too small, place a mirror inside the room to help the ch'i in; if it is too big, a wind chime or another object hanging from the ceiling will help slow down the ch'i as it rushes out.

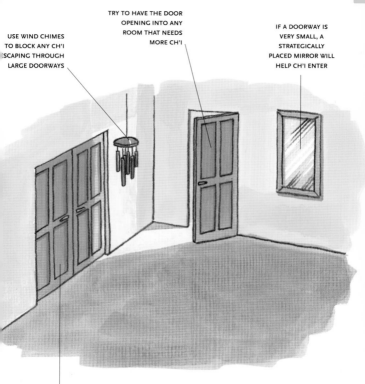

TRY TO HAVE THE DOOR
OPENING INTO ANY
ROOM THAT NEEDS
MORE CH'I

USE WIND CHIMES
TO BLOCK ANY CH'I
ESCAPING THROUGH
LARGE DOORWAYS

IF A DOORWAY IS
VERY SMALL, A
STRATEGICALLY
PLACED MIRROR WILL
HELP CH'I ENTER

ALL DOORS SHOULD
BE IN PROPORTION TO
THE ROOM SIZE

Above: **There are lots of
ways to encourage ch'i
through doors and create
a good feng shui room.**

The Feng Shui Yard

In a feng shui yard, there should be a place to sit in contemplation; a place to eat in peace; hidden areas for surprise, excitement, and intimacy; and walkways to stroll through. Compost heaps, trash cans, and fuel stores should all be hidden — screen them with trellis covered in climbers if you can, or grow shrubs in front of them if you can't.

Above: **In today's busy world, the yard is a sanctuary as well as a place for fun and relaxation.**

The ideal shape for a feng shui yard would be a square containing octagonal flower beds and/or a lawn with a circular pond in the center – with a fountain, of course.

Even if you only have a small patio, an interesting and visually stimulating space can still be created to help the overall feng shui of your home. Plant climbers to cover brickwork

Below: **Ideally, a feng shui garden would have a rectangular shape with octagonal flower beds and a circular pond.**

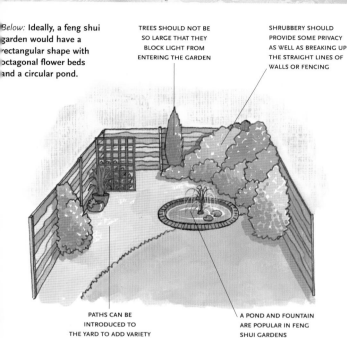

TREES SHOULD NOT BE SO LARGE THAT THEY BLOCK LIGHT FROM ENTERING THE GARDEN

SHRUBBERY SHOULD PROVIDE SOME PRIVACY AS WELL AS BREAKING UP THE STRAIGHT LINES OF WALLS OR FENCING

PATHS CAN BE INTRODUCED TO THE YARD TO ADD VARIETY

A POND AND FOUNTAIN ARE POPULAR IN FENG SHUI GARDENS

Create an "arbor" with a seat and a simple archway with plants growing up and over it — try a camomile or thyme seat and enjoy the lovely scent. Try planting herbs in wooden tubs for good feng shui and for cooking.

The main thing to remember with a courtyard or deck is not to neglect it. Sweep it regularly and keep it neat. Courtyards are usually square-shaped, so try breaking up the corners with pots, climbers, or statues.

Feng Shui Roads and Driveways

The road to the front of your house is considered very important by feng shui practitioners — it tells the world all about you. Ideally, it should curve gently, bringing your guests to you in harmony and health.

Too straight or direct a road will channel your guests into your home too quickly, and they will feel rushed and ill at ease. The road can be seen as a ch'i funnel — too straight and it will only encourage sha.

Below: **More and more modern homes include feng shui rules in their design.**

Imagine you are the ch'i – what effect will you have? Ideally, you should be looking for a wide curving road that swings around toward the house from the southeast. Your driveway should slope away gently. If it is too

THIS CURVED
DRIVEWAY IS
TRULY FENG SHUI

A LARGE AND
BRIGHTLY COLORED
FRONT DOOR ADDS
TO THIS FENG
SHUI HOME

A ROAD THAT SWINGS
TOWARD THE HOUSE
FROM THE SOUTHEAST
IS IDEAL

steep, luck and money, it is said, will roll away. Install posts or pillars just before the drive drops away too steeply to remedy this. A light placed here will also help. Horseshoe-shaped drives are very good feng shui, allowing the ch'i to arrive and depart harmoniously.

Above: **The best feng shui driveway is horse-shoe shaped with a gentle incline up to the house.**

Index